Black Soul Mirror Notebook

Images by Zara Watson-Ellis

First Printing: 2015

ISBN: 978-1-326-60842-2

Published by Faulks Books

The Seshen School of Hermetic Meditation is an online school for those following the works of Franz Bardon.

Please visit www.martinfaulks.com for more details.

SCORE CHART FOR THE ELEMENTS

Introduction

The Black Soul Mirror notebook is designed to assist you, the practitioner, in the further development and refinement of your character. Used in conjunction with the White Soul Mirror, the purpose of the Back Soul Mirror is to bring transformation to the negative vices and shortcomings pertaining to each element into positive qualities to aid you and the world around you. This allows you to investigate and explore aspects of this nature in order to achieve a balance of the four elements. As you work through this notebook, the patterns to the Black Soul Mirror will also expand your self-knowledge and allow you to discover the areas in need of development that may as of yet not be known to you. The contents of the Black Soul Mirror should be viewed as a battery of unreleased potential ready to be utilized.

The elements are listed in the following order: Earth, Water, Air and Fire. Each element is further divided into three sections, to begin with the smallest quality, then medium, and finally largest.

Within the Black Soul Mirror the focus of each elemental section is to record the negative qualities and unproductive forms of self-expression specific to the element that have been identified. Specifically, these include ineffective strategies, weaknesses and actions that cause disharmony or unnecessary pain.

First Section - Small Qualities

These pertain to shortcomings that are of a day to day occurrence that bring confusion or disharmony to a situation and thus have a small, negative impact on our lives. An example of a small, negative Earth element quality would be a tendency to put things off that need to be done.

Second Section – Medium Qualities

These are vices of a larger nature which not only hinder our own lives significantly, but also harm others. A medium Air quality would be using insults and words to belittle and put others down in order to gain control.

Third Section – Large Qualities

These could be vices that you have very little control over, that have a large negative effect on the lives of others and oneself, for example the tendency to lose ones temper and become irresponsible could be seen as a large vice of the Fire element.

Attributing Scores to the Elements

Once the appropriate qualities have been added to the Soul Mirror, it is necessary to attribute a collective score to each element, see fig. 1 for example. Thus allowing a greater assessment of the traits and an

insight into which element is most prominent, aiding you in the development of equipoise.

Method of Scoring
A suggested method of scoring, is to add a number based on the quality and quantity attributed to that particular vice. For example,

1= Small Qualities

2= Medium Qualities

3= Large Qualities

Once the negative qualities and vices have been added next to the appropriate element and a score attributed to each one of them, total up the scores for each element and record them on the score sheet provided at the front of the book. This will provide a useful insight into which element is predominant within your personality and assist in a greater understanding of oneself.

Fig. 1 Example Score Chart

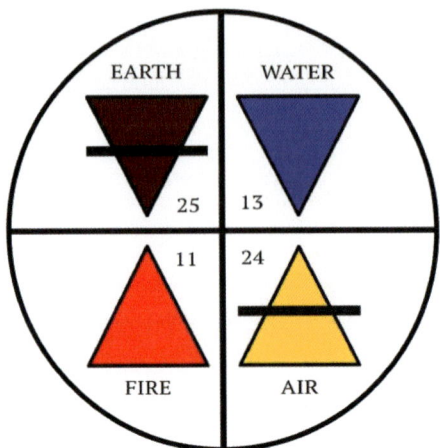

EARTH ELEMENT

SMALL NEGATIVE QUALITIES

EARTH ELEMENT

SMALL NEGATIVE QUALITIES

EARTH ELEMENT

SMALL NEGATIVE QUALITIES

EARTH ELEMENT

SMALL NEGATIVE QUALITIES

EARTH ELEMENT

SMALL NEGATIVE QUALITIES

EARTH ELEMENT

SMALL NEGATIVE QUALITIES

EARTH ELEMENT

SMALL NEGATIVE QUALITIES

EARTH ELEMENT

SMALL NEGATIVE QUALITIES

EARTH ELEMENT

SMALL NEGATIVE QUALITIES

EARTH ELEMENT

SMALL NEGATIVE QUALITIES

EARTH ELEMENT

MEDIUM NEGATIVE QUALITIES

EARTH ELEMENT

MEDIUM NEGATIVE QUALITIES

EARTH ELEMENT

MEDIUM NEGATIVE QUALITIES

EARTH ELEMENT

MEDIUM NEGATIVE QUALITIES

EARTH ELEMENT

MEDIUM NEGATIVE QUALITIES

EARTH ELEMENT

MEDIUM NEGATIVE QUALITIES

EARTH ELEMENT

MEDIUM NEGATIVE QUALITIES

EARTH ELEMENT

MEDIUM NEGATIVE QUALITIES

EARTH ELEMENT

MEDIUM NEGATIVE QUALITIES

EARTH ELEMENT

LARGE NEGATIVE QUALITIES

EARTH ELEMENT

LARGE NEGATIVE QUALITIES

EARTH ELEMENT

LARGE NEGATIVE QUALITIES

EARTH ELEMENT

LARGE NEGATIVE QUALITIES

EARTH ELEMENT

LARGE NEGATIVE QUALITIES

EARTH ELEMENT

LARGE NEGATIVE QUALITIES

EARTH ELEMENT

LARGE NEGATIVE QUALITIES

EARTH ELEMENT

LARGE NEGATIVE QUALITIES

EARTH ELEMENT

LARGE NEGATIVE QUALITIES

EARTH ELEMENT

LARGE NEGATIVE QUALITIES

WATER ELEMENT

SMALL NEGATIVE QUALITIES

WATER ELEMENT

SMALL NEGATIVE QUALITIES

WATER ELEMENT

SMALL NEGATIVE QUALITIES

WATER ELEMENT

SMALL NEGATIVE QUALITIES

WATER ELEMENT

SMALL NEGATIVE QUALITIES

WATER ELEMENT

SMALL NEGATIVE QUALITIES

WATER ELEMENT

SMALL NEGATIVE QUALITIES

WATER ELEMENT

SMALL NEGATIVE QUALITIES

WATER ELEMENT

SMALL NEGATIVE QUALITIES

WATER ELEMENT

SMALL NEGATIVE QUALITIES

WATER ELEMENT

MEDIUM NEGATIVE QUALITIES

WATER ELEMENT

MEDIUM NEGATIVE QUALITIES

WATER ELEMENT

MEDIUM NEGATIVE QUALITIES

WATER ELEMENT

MEDIUM NEGATIVE QUALITIES

WATER ELEMENT

MEDIUM NEGATIVE QUALITIES

WATER ELEMENT

MEDIUM NEGATIVE QUALITIES

WATER ELEMENT

MEDIUM NEGATIVE QUALITIES

WATER ELEMENT

MEDIUM NEGATIVE QUALITIES

WATER ELEMENT

MEDIUM NEGATIVE QUALITIES

WATER ELEMENT

MEDIUM NEGATIVE QUALITIES

WATER ELEMENT

LARGE NEGATIVE QUALITIES

WATER ELEMENT

LARGE NEGATIVE QUALITIES

WATER ELEMENT

LARGE NEGATIVE QUALITIES

WATER ELEMENT

LARGE NEGATIVE QUALITIES

WATER ELEMENT

LARGE NEGATIVE QUALITIES

WATER ELEMENT

LARGE NEGATIVE QUALITIES

WATER ELEMENT

LARGE NEGATIVE QUALITIES

WATER ELEMENT

LARGE NEGATIVE QUALITIES

WATER ELEMENT

LARGE NEGATIVE QUALITIES

WATER ELEMENT

LARGE NEGATIVE QUALITIES

AIR ELEMENT

SMALL NEGATIVE QUALITIES

AIR ELEMENT

SMALL NEGATIVE QUALITIES

AIR ELEMENT

SMALL NEGATIVE QUALITIES

AIR ELEMENT

SMALL NEGATIVE QUALITIES

AIR ELEMENT

SMALL NEGATIVE QUALITIES

AIR ELEMENT

SMALL NEGATIVE QUALITIES

AIR ELEMENT

SMALL NEGATIVE QUALITIES

AIR ELEMENT

SMALL NEGATIVE QUALITIES

AIR ELEMENT

SMALL NEGATIVE QUALITIES

AIR ELEMENT

SMALL NEGATIVE QUALITIES

AIR ELEMENT

MEDIUM NEGATIVE QUALITIES

AIR ELEMENT

MEDIUM NEGATIVE QUALITIES

AIR ELEMENT

MEDIUM NEGATIVE QUALITIES

AIR ELEMENT

MEDIUM NEGATIVE QUALITIES

AIR ELEMENT

MEDIUM NEGATIVE QUALITIES

AIR ELEMENT

MEDIUM NEGATIVE QUALITIES

AIR ELEMENT

MEDIUM NEGATIVE QUALITIES

AIR ELEMENT

MEDIUM NEGATIVE QUALITIES

AIR ELEMENT

MEDIUM NEGATIVE QUALITIES

AIR ELEMENT

MEDIUM NEGATIVE QUALITIES

AIR ELEMENT

LARGE NEGATIVE QUALITIES

AIR ELEMENT

LARGE NEGATIVE QUALITIES

AIR ELEMENT

LARGE NEGATIVE QUALITIES

AIR ELEMENT

LARGE NEGATIVE QUALITIES

AIR ELEMENT

LARGE NEGATIVE QUALITIES

AIR ELEMENT

LARGE NEGATIVE QUALITIES

AIR ELEMENT

LARGE NEGATIVE QUALITIES

AIR ELEMENT

LARGE NEGATIVE QUALITIES

AIR ELEMENT

LARGE NEGATIVE QUALITIES

AIR ELEMENT

LARGE NEGATIVE QUALITIES

FIRE ELEMENT

SMALL NEGATIVE QUALITIES

FIRE ELEMENT

SMALL NEGATIVE QUALITIES

FIRE ELEMENT

SMALL NEGATIVE QUALITIES

FIRE ELEMENT

SMALL NEGATIVE QUALITIES

FIRE ELEMENT

SMALL NEGATIVE QUALITIES

FIRE ELEMENT

SMALL NEGATIVE QUALITIES

FIRE ELEMENT

SMALL NEGATIVE QUALITIES

FIRE ELEMENT

SMALL NEGATIVE QUALITIES

FIRE ELEMENT

SMALL NEGATIVE QUALITIES

FIRE ELEMENT

SMALL NEGATIVE QUALITIES

FIRE ELEMENT

MEDIUM NEGATIVE QUALITIES

FIRE ELEMENT

MEDIUM NEGATIVE QUALITIES

FIRE ELEMENT

MEDIUM NEGATIVE QUALITIES

FIRE ELEMENT

MEDIUM NEGATIVE QUALITIES

FIRE ELEMENT

MEDIUM NEGATIVE QUALITIES

FIRE ELEMENT

MEDIUM NEGATIVE QUALITIES

FIRE ELEMENT

MEDIUM NEGATIVE QUALITIES

FIRE ELEMENT

MEDIUM NEGATIVE QUALITIES

FIRE ELEMENT

MEDIUM NEGATIVE QUALITIES

FIRE ELEMENT

MEDIUM NEGATIVE QUALITIES

FIRE ELEMENT

LARGE NEGATIVE QUALITIES

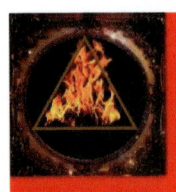

FIRE ELEMENT

LARGE NEGATIVE QUALITIES

FIRE ELEMENT

LARGE NEGATIVE QUALITIES

FIRE ELEMENT

LARGE NEGATIVE QUALITIES

FIRE ELEMENT

LARGE NEGATIVE QUALITIES

FIRE ELEMENT

LARGE NEGATIVE QUALITIES

FIRE ELEMENT

LARGE NEGATIVE QUALITIES

FIRE ELEMENT

LARGE NEGATIVE QUALITIES

FIRE ELEMENT

LARGE NEGATIVE QUALITIES

FIRE ELEMENT

LARGE NEGATIVE QUALITIES

15604631R00075

Printed in Germany
by Amazon
Distribution